CONTENTS

PROLOGUE: MY JOURNEY INTO SWIFTUI

Hi, I'm Shubhayan , a iOS Tech Lead with years of experience in building mobile applications. My journey in iOS development has taken me through the evolution of Apple's ecosystem—from UIKit's imperative approach to the declarative power of SwiftUI. As a Tech Lead in MNCs , I've helped deliver high-quality products, guided teams, and supported clients in making key architectural decisions.

Beyond development, I also contribute as a **Subject Matter Expert (SME) for iOS interviews**, helping organizations find the right talent. Over the years, I've worked on various projects, from research apps collecting vital health data to integrating complex architectures like MVVM, VIPER, and SOLID principles into real-world applications.

This book is written **for beginners**—for those stepping into SwiftUI for the first time, looking for a structured and practical approach to learning. Unlike other resources that mix SwiftUI with Combine or advanced patterns too soon, my goal is to provide **a solid foundation** in SwiftUI alone. From UI basics to MVVM architecture, this book will guide you step by step, ensuring that by the end, you can confidently build your own SwiftUI applications.

As a bonus, I've also included **SwiftUI interview Q&A**, based on my experience in technical hiring. Whether you're preparing for job interviews or just want to strengthen your fundamentals, these questions will give you an edge.

Let's dive into the world of **SwiftUI**, where building iOS apps has never been more intuitive and efficient.

INTRODUCTION: YOUR FIRST STEP INTO SWIFTUI

SwiftUI is Apple's **modern UI framework** that makes building iOS apps **faster, easier, and more intuitive**. If you've ever struggled with **Auto Layout, Storyboards, or UIKit**, SwiftUI is here to change the game!

This book is designed for **absolute beginners**, guiding you through the **core concepts of SwiftUI** step by step. By the end, you'll be able to **build real-world apps** using SwiftUI's declarative syntax and **understand how to structure your app using MVVM architecture**.

Why This Book?

 Simple & Beginner-Friendly → No prior SwiftUI experience needed.

 Step-by-Step Learning → Covers everything from **basic UI components to MVVM and API calls**.

 Interview Prep Bonus → Includes a **SwiftUI Q&A section** to help you crack iOS interviews.

What You'll Learn in This Book

 Chapter 1: SwiftUI Basics → How SwiftUI differs from UIKit, working with **Views, Modifiers, and Bindings**.

 Chapter 2: UI Components in SwiftUI → Learn **HStack, VStack, ZStack, ScrollView, Spacer**, and more.

▢ **Chapter 3: State Management** → Master @State, @Binding, and @EnvironmentObject.

▢ **Chapter 4: MVVM in SwiftUI** → Build a **clean and structured** SwiftUI app.

▢ **Chapter 5: Networking with SOLID Principles** → Fetch and display API data with **maintainable code**.

▢ **Bonus: SwiftUI Q&A for Interviews** → Get ready for **SwiftUI interview questions** with clear answers!

By the end of this book, you'll have a **solid foundation in SwiftUI** and the confidence to **build, structure, and optimize iOS apps**.

Ready to master SwiftUI? Let's get started! ▢

What is SwiftUI and How Does it Differ from UIKit?

SwiftUI is a declarative framework introduced by Apple to build user interfaces (UI) across all Apple platforms (iOS, macOS, watchOS, and tvOS). SwiftUI allows developers to describe what the UI should look like for a given state, and it takes care of updating the interface when the data changes.

In contrast, **UIKit** is the older, imperative framework for building UIs in iOS apps. With UIKit, developers must manually manage UI updates and handle state changes, which often results in more boilerplate code and complex logic. SwiftUI simplifies this by being declarative—meaning you describe the UI in terms of its state, and SwiftUI manages the underlying changes.

SwiftUI vs UIKit: Key Differences

- **Declarative vs Imperative**:
  - In SwiftUI, you declare what the UI should look like based on the current state.
  - In UIKit, you need to tell the system how to change the UI, often with complex logic and event handlers.

- **Automatic UI Updates**:
    - SwiftUI automatically updates the UI when the state changes, without needing to manually call methods like setNeedsLayout or reloadData in UIKit.
- **Code Conciseness**:
    - SwiftUI reduces the amount of code you need to write compared to UIKit, especially for creating and managing views.

BASIC CONCEPTS
IN SWIFTUI

1. Views

In SwiftUI, everything on the screen is a View. A view represents a part of the user interface (UI) that can be displayed, and it can contain other views. Views are composed of structures (structs) that conform to the View protocol.

Here's a simple example of a Text view in SwiftUI:

```
import SwiftUI

struct ContentView: View {
  var body: some View {
    Text("Hello, SwiftUI!")
      .font(.largeTitle)
      .padding()
  }
}
```

In this example:

- Text is a basic SwiftUI view that displays text.
- .font() and .padding() are **modifiers** (we'll cover this next).

2. Modifiers

Modifiers in SwiftUI are used to apply changes to views, such as changing the color, size, or alignment. Each modifier returns a new view with the modifications applied.

Example of using multiple modifiers:

```
import SwiftUI

struct ContentView: View {
  var body: some View {
```

```
    Text("Hello, SwiftUI!")
        .font(.title)
        .foregroundColor(.blue) // Modifier to change the text color
        .padding(20)        // Modifier to add padding around text
        .background(Color.yellow) // Modifier to set background color
        .cornerRadius(10)     // Modifier to round the corners
    }
}
```

Here, Text is modified by:

- .font(.title): Sets the font size.
- .foregroundColor(.blue): Sets the text color.
- .padding(20): Adds padding around the text.
- .background(Color.yellow): Adds a yellow background.
- .cornerRadius(10): Rounds the corners of the background.

3. Bindings

A Binding in SwiftUI is a reference to a value that allows you to read and write the value. It's used for creating **two-way data binding** between a view and the model. Bindings are often used with controls like sliders, text fields, and toggles, where you want to update the model when the user interacts with the UI.

Here's an example of a Binding with a Toggle:

```
import SwiftUI

struct ContentView: View {
    @State private var isToggled: Bool = false

    var body: some View {
        VStack {
            Toggle("Enable Feature", isOn: $isToggled)
                .padding()

            Text(isToggled ? "Feature is Enabled" : "Feature is Disabled")
                .padding()
                .foregroundColor(isToggled ? .green : .red)
        }
```

```
    }
}
```

In this example:

- @State is a property wrapper that allows SwiftUI to manage the state of the isToggled variable.
- $isToggled is a Binding, passed to the Toggle to reflect changes both ways—when the toggle is changed, isToggled updates, and when isToggled changes, the UI updates.
- The Text view changes dynamically based on the state of isToggled.

Simple SwiftUI Example: Building a Counter App

Let's put these concepts together with a simple **counter app** that increases a number each time a button is pressed.

```swift
import SwiftUI

struct ContentView: View {
    @State private var count = 0 // State to store the count

    var body: some View {
        VStack {
            Text("Counter: \(count)") // Display the count
                .font(.largeTitle)
                .padding()

            Button(action: {
                count += 1 // Increment the count when button is pressed
            }) {
                Text("Increase Count")
                    .padding()
                    .background(Color.blue)
                    .foregroundColor(.white)
                    .cornerRadius(10)
            }
        }
        .padding()
    }
}
```

Explanation:

- @State private var count = 0: The state that tracks the counter.

- Text("Counter: \(count)"): A Text view displays the current counter value.
- Button(action: {...}): A Button view that triggers the action to increase the count when pressed.
- .padding(), .background(), .foregroundColor(), .cornerRadius(): Modifiers that add styling to the text and button.

Conclusion

SwiftUI offers a modern, declarative way to build user interfaces. Unlike UIKit, which requires you to manage views and their state imperatively, SwiftUI simplifies UI updates by binding views directly to their state. Modifiers let you easily customize views, while Binding allows you to maintain two-way communication between the view and model.

By understanding these core concepts—**Views**, **Modifiers**, and **Bindings**—you can begin building simple and powerful user interfaces in SwiftUI. The real power of SwiftUI comes when these components are used together to create reactive, dynamic applications that update automatically in response to state changes.

Understanding @State, @Binding, and @EnvironmentObject in SwiftUI

SwiftUI provides property wrappers like @State, @Binding, and @EnvironmentObject to manage and share data between views efficiently. These wrappers ensure that the UI updates dynamically when the underlying data changes. Let's explore each one in detail.

---

1. @State: Managing Local State in a View

What is @State?

@State is a property wrapper used to manage **local mutable state** within a SwiftUI view. When a @State variable changes, SwiftUI automatically re-renders the view.

Key points about @State:

- It's **private** to the view in which it is declared.
- SwiftUI manages the memory and updates the UI automatically when its value changes.
- Used for simple state values like booleans, numbers, and text.

Example: A Simple Counter Using @State

```
import SwiftUI

struct CounterView: View {
    @State private var count = 0 // Local state variable

    var body: some View {
        VStack {
            Text("Counter: \(count)")
                .font(.largeTitle)
                .padding()

            Button("Increase Count") {
                count += 1 // Updating @State will refresh the view
            }
            .padding()
            .background(Color.blue)
            .foregroundColor(.white)
```

```
        .cornerRadius(10)
      }
   }
}
```

How it works:

- @State private var count = 0: A state variable that holds the count.
- When the **button is tapped**, count += 1 updates the state.
- SwiftUI **automatically re-renders** the UI with the new count value.

2. @Binding: Passing a State Variable to Another View

What is @Binding?

@Binding allows a **child view** to modify a state variable owned by its **parent view**. This creates a **two-way connection**, meaning the child can read and write the parent's state.

Key points about @Binding:

- It **does not own the data** but gets a reference to the parent's state.
- Used when a child view needs to modify a state variable from the parent.

Example: Parent-Child Communication Using @Binding

```
import SwiftUI

struct ParentView: View {
   @State private var isOn = false // Parent owns the state

   var body: some View {
      VStack {
         Toggle("Enable Feature", isOn: $isOn) // Direct @State binding
            .padding()

         ToggleView(isOn: $isOn) // Passing state to child using @Binding
      }
   }
```

```
}
struct ToggleView: View {
    @Binding var isOn: Bool  // Child gets @Binding reference

    var body: some View {
        VStack {
            Toggle("Child Toggle", isOn: $isOn)
                .padding()
            Text(isOn ? "Feature is ON" : "Feature is OFF")
        }
    }
}
```

How it works:

1. The **parent view (ParentView)** has an @State variable isOn.
2. The **child view (ToggleView)** receives isOn as a @Binding, allowing it to modify the parent's state.
3. Changing the toggle in **either view updates both**, because they share the same underlying data.

---

3. @EnvironmentObject: Sharing Data Across Multiple Views

What is @EnvironmentObject?

@EnvironmentObject is used to **share data across multiple views** without passing it manually. It is particularly useful for **global app state management**.

Key points about @EnvironmentObject:

- It allows **any child view** in the hierarchy to access the same object.
- Useful for app-wide state, such as user authentication, settings, or data models.
- Requires an **ObservableObject** to store the shared data.

Example: Managing User Settings with @EnvironmentObject

Step 1: Create a Shared ObservableObject

import SwiftUI

```
class UserSettings: ObservableObject {
    @Published var username: String = "Guest"  // Data to be shared
}
```

Step 2: Provide the EnvironmentObject in the Root View

```
@main
struct MyApp: App {
    @StateObject var settings = UserSettings()  // Create shared instance

    var body: some Scene {
        WindowGroup {
            ParentView()
                .environmentObject(settings)  // Inject into environment
        }
    }
}
```

Step 3: Access @EnvironmentObject in Views

```
struct ParentView: View {
    var body: some View {
        VStack {
            ChildView()
        }
    }
}

struct ChildView: View {
    @EnvironmentObject var settings: UserSettings  // Access shared object

    var body: some View {
        VStack {
            Text("Username: \(settings.username)")
                .font(.title)

            Button("Change Username") {
                settings.username = "Swift Developer"  // Updates all views
            }
            .padding()
            .background(Color.blue)
            .foregroundColor(.white)
            .cornerRadius(10)
        }
        .padding()
    }
}
```

How it works:

1. **UserSettings** is an ObservableObject that holds the username property.
2. **@StateObject var settings = UserSettings()** creates the shared state.
3. **.environmentObject(settings)** makes the object available to all views.
4. **Child views use** @EnvironmentObject to access and modify the shared data.
5. When the **username changes**, all views using it **update automatically**.

When to Use @State, @Binding, and @EnvironmentObject

Property Wrapper	Used For	Owned By	Example
@State	**Local state within a single view**	The view itself	Counter, toggle states
@Binding	**Passing state to child views**	Parent view	A child modifying a parent's state
@EnvironmentObject	**Global state shared across multiple views**	A shared data model	User settings, app-wide state

Combining @State, @Binding, and @EnvironmentObject Together

Here's an example integrating all three concepts.

```
import SwiftUI

class SettingsManager: ObservableObject {
    @Published var isDarkMode: Bool = false
}

struct ParentView: View {
    @State private var username: String = "Guest"
```

```swift
@StateObject var settings = SettingsManager()

var body: some View {
    VStack {
        Text("Hello, \(username)!")
            .font(.largeTitle)

        ChildView(username: $username) // Using @Binding

        Toggle("Dark Mode", isOn: $settings.isDarkMode)
            .padding()

        NavigationLink("Go to Settings", destination: SettingsView())
    }
    .environmentObject(settings) // Provide EnvironmentObject
}
}
struct ChildView: View {
    @Binding var username: String

    var body: some View {
        TextField("Enter Name", text: $username)
            .textFieldStyle(RoundedBorderTextFieldStyle())
            .padding()
    }
}

struct SettingsView: View {
    @EnvironmentObject var settings: SettingsManager

    var body: some View {
        VStack {
            Text("Dark Mode is \(settings.isDarkMode ? "ON" : "OFF")")
            Toggle("Enable Dark Mode", isOn: $settings.isDarkMode)
                .padding()
        }
    }
}
```

How it Works:

1. @State manages local state (username).
2. @Binding allows ChildView to modify the username.
3. @StateObject initializes the SettingsManager.
4. @EnvironmentObject makes SettingsManager accessible in SettingsView.

Conclusion

- @State is used for **local state** within a view.
- @Binding allows a **child view** to modify the parent's state.
- @EnvironmentObject is used for **global shared state** across multiple views.
- Using these effectively allows for a **clean, maintainable, and reactive** SwiftUI architecture.

SWIFTUI LAYOUT COMPONENTS: HSTACK, VSTACK, SPACER, AND SCROLLVIEW

SwiftUI provides flexible layout containers to arrange views horizontally, vertically, and manage spacing efficiently. Understanding these components is crucial for building responsive and adaptive UIs.

1. HStack (Horizontal Stack)

What is HStack?

HStack arranges views **horizontally** from **left to right**.

Basic Example

```
HStack {
    Text("Left")
    Text("Center")
    Text("Right")
}
```

⬜ This will display:

Left Center Right

Example with Spacing and Alignment

```
HStack(spacing: 20) {
    Text("Swift")
```

```
    Text("UI")
    Text("Rocks!")
}
.alignmentGuide(.bottom) { _ in 10 } // Aligning text
```

☐ spacing: 20 adds **space between items**.

Example with Images and Icons

```
HStack {
    Image(systemName: "star.fill")
        .foregroundColor(.yellow)
    Text("Favorites")
}
```

☐ You can mix **text, images, and buttons** inside an HStack.

2. VStack (Vertical Stack)

What is VStack?

VStack arranges views **vertically** from **top to bottom**.

Basic Example

```
VStack {
    Text("First")
    Text("Second")
    Text("Third")
}
```

☐ Displays:

First
Second
Third

Example with Alignment and Spacing

```
VStack(alignment: .leading, spacing: 15) {
    Text("Hello")
    Text("SwiftUI")
    Text("World")
}
```

☐ alignment: .leading aligns content **to the left**.

Example: VStack with Buttons

```
VStack {
    Button("Sign Up") { print("Sign Up tapped") }
    Button("Login") { print("Login tapped") }
}
```

☐ VStack is **great for vertical button layouts.**

3. Spacer (Flexible Empty Space)

What is Spacer?

Spacer **pushes views apart** by taking up available space.

Example: Centered Text

```
HStack {
    Spacer()
    Text("Centered")
    Spacer()
}
```

☐ Spacer() ensures the text stays in the **center.**

Example: Bottom-Aligned Button

```
VStack {
    Text("Some Content")
    Spacer() // Pushes button to bottom
    Button("Continue") { }
}
```

☐ Spacer() **pushes the button to the bottom.**

4. ScrollView (Scrollable Content)

What is ScrollView?

ScrollView **enables scrolling** for large content.

Basic Vertical ScrollView

```
ScrollView {
    VStack {
        ForEach(1...20, id: \.self) { index in
            Text("Item \(index)")
                .padding()
                .background(Color.gray.opacity(0.2))
                .cornerRadius(10)
        }
    }
}
```

☐ This creates a **scrollable list of items.**

Horizontal ScrollView

```
ScrollView(.horizontal) {
    HStack {
        ForEach(1...10, id: \.self) { index in
            Text("Item \(index)")
                .padding()
                .background(Color.blue)
                .cornerRadius(10)
        }
    }
}
```

☐ This enables **horizontal scrolling.**

Combining HStack, VStack, Spacer, and ScrollView

Example: A Profile Card Layout

```
VStack {
    Image(systemName: "person.circle.fill")
        .resizable()
        .frame(width: 100, height: 100)

    Text("John Doe")
        .font(.title)

    Text("iOS Developer")
        .foregroundColor(.gray)

    Spacer()

    ScrollView {
        VStack(alignment: .leading) {
            Text("Bio")
                .font(.headline)
            Text("Lorem ipsum dolor sit amet...")
        }
        .padding()
    }
}
.padding()
```

☐ **Combining VStack, Spacer, and ScrollView** creates a clean **profile screen.**

Conclusion

- HStack → **Horizontal layouts**
- VStack → **Vertical layouts**
- Spacer → **Pushes views apart**
- ScrollView → **Scrollable content**

MVVM ARCHITECTURE
IN SWIFTUI

What is MVVM?

MVVM (Model-View-ViewModel) is a **design pattern** that separates UI logic from business logic. It makes code **cleaner, reusable, and testable**.

MVVM Breakdown:

1. **Model** → Represents the data and business logic.
2. **ViewModel** → Handles the logic and state, acting as a bridge between Model and View.
3. **View** → The UI that displays data from the ViewModel.

---

1 Creating a Simple MVVM Example

Step 1: Model (Data Structure)

Define a simple User model:

```
struct User {
    let id: Int
    let name: String
    let age: Int
}
```

Step 2: ViewModel (Data Handling)

Create a UserViewModel to manage user data:

```
import SwiftUI

class UserViewModel: ObservableObject {
    @Published var users: [User] = [] // Updates UI when changed
```

```
init() {
    fetchUsers()
}

func fetchUsers() {
    users = [
        User(id: 1, name: "Alice", age: 25),
        User(id: 2, name: "Bob", age: 30),
        User(id: 3, name: "Charlie", age: 35)
    ]
}
}
```

☐ @Published ensures updates to users reflect in the UI.
☐ ObservableObject allows SwiftUI views to observe changes.

Step 3: View (UI)

Now, create a SwiftUI UserListView:

```
import SwiftUI

struct UserListView: View {
    @StateObject var viewModel = UserViewModel()  // Connects ViewModel to View

    var body: some View {
        List(viewModel.users, id: \.id) { user in
            VStack(alignment: .leading) {
                Text(user.name)
                    .font(.headline)
                Text("Age: \(user.age)")
                    .font(.subheadline)
            }
        }
        .navigationTitle("Users")
    }
}
```

☐ @StateObject initializes and manages the ViewModel.
☐ List displays dynamic data from viewModel.users.

2 Understanding @State, @Binding, @EnvironmentObject in MVVM

@State
Used for **local state** inside a View.
Example:

```
struct CounterView: View {
    @State private var count = 0  // Local state

    var body: some View {
        VStack {
            Text("Count: \(count)")
            Button("Increment") { count += 1 }
        }
    }
}
```

@Binding
Used for **sharing state** between parent and child views.
Example:

```
struct ParentView: View {
    @State private var isOn = false

    var body: some View {
        ToggleView(isOn: $isOn)
    }
}

struct ToggleView: View {
    @Binding var isOn: Bool  // Receives value from ParentView

    var body: some View {
        Toggle("Switch", isOn: $isOn)
    }
}
```

☐ Changes in ToggleView reflect in ParentView.

@EnvironmentObject
Used for **global state sharing** across multiple views.
Example:

```
class SettingsViewModel: ObservableObject {
    @Published var isDarkMode = false
}

@main
```

```
struct MyApp: App {
  @StateObject var settings = SettingsViewModel()

  var body: some Scene {
    WindowGroup {
      ContentView()
        .environmentObject(settings) // Inject ViewModel globally
    }
  }
}

struct ContentView: View {
  @EnvironmentObject var settings: SettingsViewModel // Access global state

  var body: some View {
    Toggle("Dark Mode", isOn: $settings.isDarkMode)
  }
}
```

☐ @EnvironmentObject allows any view to access settings.

3 Adding Networking to ViewModel

Let's fetch real data from an API using URLSession.

Update ViewModel to Fetch API Data

```
import SwiftUI

class UserViewModel: ObservableObject {
  @Published var users: [User] = []

  func fetchUsers() {
    guard let url = URL(string: "https://jsonplaceholder.typicode.com/users")
    else { return }

    URLSession.shared.dataTask(with: url) { data, _, error in
      guard let data = data, error == nil else { return }

      DispatchQueue.main.async {
        self.users = (try? JSONDecoder().decode([User].self, from: data)) ??
        []
      }
    }.resume()
  }
}
```

☐ Fetches data from a fake API and updates users.
☐ Uses DispatchQueue.main.async to update UI.

4 Conclusion

☐ **MVVM** **separates** **concerns**, making the code more maintainable.

☐ **ViewModel manages data**, so the UI remains simple.

☐ Use @State, @Binding, and @EnvironmentObject **to manage state effectively**.

☐ **Networking inside ViewModel** helps fetch real-time data.

SOLID PRINCIPLES IN SWIFTUI NETWORK CALLS

What is SOLID?

SOLID is a set of five principles that make code **scalable, maintainable, and testable**. Let's apply it to a **networking layer in SwiftUI using MVVM.**

1. S - Single Responsibility Principle (SRP)

Each class should have **only one reason to change.**

☐ **Solution** → Separate **Networking, Models,** and **ViewModels.**

2. O - Open/Closed Principle (OCP)

Code should be **open for extension but closed for modification.**

☐ **Solution** → Use **protocols** to allow different API services without modifying existing code.

3. L - Liskov Substitution Principle (LSP)

Subclasses should be **replaceable** without breaking the program.

☐ **Solution** → Use **protocol-based abstraction** for network calls.

4. I - Interface Segregation Principle (ISP)

Don't force classes to **implement unnecessary methods.**

☐ **Solution** → Define **small, focused protocols.**

5. D - Dependency Inversion Principle (DIP)

High-level modules **should not depend on low-level modules.**

☐ **Solution** → Use **dependency injection** to pass dependencies instead of hardcoding them.

☐ Applying SOLID to a Simple SwiftUI Networking Example

Step 1: Define the Model

First, we create a simple User model that represents API data:

```
struct User: Codable, Identifiable {
    let id: Int
    let name: String
    let email: String
}
```

Step 2: Create a Networking Protocol

☐ This ensures flexibility by allowing different networking implementations.

```
protocol NetworkService {
    func fetchUsers(completion: @escaping (Result<[User], Error>) -> Void)
}
```

☐ The protocol enforces that any **networking class** must implement fetchUsers().

Step 3: Implement the API Service

☐ This follows **SRP** by keeping the network logic separate.

```
import Foundation

class APIService: NetworkService {
    func fetchUsers(completion: @escaping (Result<[User], Error>) -> Void) {
        guard let url = URL(string: "https://jsonplaceholder.typicode.com/users")
        else {
            completion(.failure(NetworkError.invalidURL))
            return
        }
```

```
URLSession.shared.dataTask(with: url) { data, _, error in
    if let error = error {
        completion(.failure(error))
        return
    }

    guard let data = data else {
        completion(.failure(NetworkError.noData))
        return
    }

    do {
        let users = try JSONDecoder().decode([User].self, from: data)
        completion(.success(users))   .
    } catch {
        completion(.failure(error))
    }
    }.resume()
  }
}

// Define Custom Errors
enum NetworkError: Error {
    case invalidURL
    case noData
}
```

☐ **OCP** → If we later switch to Alamofire, we just add another class without modifying existing code.

Step 4: ViewModel with Dependency Injection

☐ This follows **DIP**, making the ViewModel independent of APIService.

```
import SwiftUI

class UserViewModel: ObservableObject {
    @Published var users: [User] = []
    private let networkService: NetworkService // Dependency Injection

    init(networkService: NetworkService) {
        self.networkService = networkService
        fetchUsers()
    }

    func fetchUsers() {
```

```
networkService.fetchUsers { [weak self] result in
    DispatchQueue.main.async {
        switch result {
        case .success(let users):
            self?.users = users
        case .failure(let error):
            print("Error fetching users: \(error)")
        }
    }
}
}
```

☐ **DIP** → UserViewModel depends on the NetworkService **protocol**, not APIService.

☐ **SRP** → UserViewModel only **manages data**. It doesn't handle API logic.

Step 5: Build the SwiftUI View

☐ This follows **MVVM** by keeping the UI logic separate.

```
import SwiftUI

struct UserListView: View {
    @StateObject var viewModel: UserViewModel

    init() {
        _viewModel = StateObject(wrappedValue: UserViewModel(networkService:
APIService()))
    }

    var body: some View {
        NavigationView {
            List(viewModel.users) { user in
                VStack(alignment: .leading) {
                    Text(user.name).font(.headline)
                    Text(user.email).font(.subheadline)
                }
            }
            .navigationTitle("Users")
        }
    }
}
```

☐ **DIP** → The UserViewModel **injects APIService**, so it's easy to swap later.

☐ **SRP** → This View only handles UI.

☐ Benefits of this Approach

☐ **Follows SOLID principles** → Code is **scalable, testable, and maintainable**.

☐ **Easy to test** → We can replace APIService with a **mock service** for unit testing.

☐ **Flexible** → We can swap APIService for another service without changing ViewModel.

Here's a **SwiftUI Interview Q&A** section that will help beginners and experienced developers prepare for job interviews.

SWIFTUI INTERVIEW Q&A

1. What is SwiftUI? How is it different from UIKit?

SwiftUI is a **declarative UI framework** introduced by Apple in iOS 13. It allows developers to build UI with **less code** and **real-time previews**.

Differences between SwiftUI & UIKit:

Feature	SwiftUI	UIKit
Syntax	Declarative	Imperative
UI Updates	Automatic with @State, @Binding	Manual with delegate & NotificationCenter
Code Reusability	High (Works on iOS, macOS, watchOS, tvOS)	Low (UIKit is iOS-specific)
Live Previews	Yes (Xcode Canvas)	No
Learning Curve	Easier for beginners	Steeper due to constraints & storyboards

2. What are @State, @Binding, and @EnvironmentObject?

These are property wrappers for **state management** in SwiftUI.

- @State: Stores **local, private** state for a view.
- @Binding: Allows a child view to **mutate a parent's state**.
- @EnvironmentObject: Shares state **globally** across multiple

views.

Example:

```
struct ParentView: View {
    @State private var counter = 0

    var body: some View {
        ChildView(counter: $counter)
    }
}

struct ChildView: View {
    @Binding var counter: Int

    var body: some View {
        VStack {
            Text("Counter: \(counter)")
            Button("Increment") {
                counter += 1
            }
        }
    }
}
```

---

3. Explain MVVM in SwiftUI. How do you implement it?

MVVM (Model-View-ViewModel) separates business logic from UI.

- **Model** → Data layer (e.g., API response, database model)
- **View** → UI layer (SwiftUI views)
- **ViewModel** → Handles business logic and updates the view

Example:

```
// Model
struct User: Identifiable {
    let id: Int
    let name: String
}

// ViewModel
class UserViewModel: ObservableObject {
    @Published var users: [User] = []
```

```swift
    func fetchUsers() {
        // Mock API Call
        users = [User(id: 1, name: "John Doe"), User(id: 2, name: "Jane Doe")]
    }
}

// View
struct UserListView: View {
    @StateObject var viewModel = UserViewModel()

    var body: some View {
        List(viewModel.users) { user in
            Text(user.name)
        }
        .onAppear {
            viewModel.fetchUsers()
        }
    }
}
```

4. How do you make a network request in SwiftUI following SOLID principles?

Follow **SOLID principles** by separating networking logic into a service layer.

Example using MVVM + SOLID:

```swift
// Model
struct Post: Decodable {
    let id: Int
    let title: String
}

// Protocol (Dependency Inversion)
protocol PostServiceProtocol {
    func fetchPosts() async throws -> [Post]
}

// Service Layer (Single Responsibility)
class PostService: PostServiceProtocol {
    func fetchPosts() async throws -> [Post] {
        guard let url = URL(string: "https://jsonplaceholder.typicode.com/posts")
else { throw URLError(.badURL) }
        let (data, _) = try await URLSession.shared.data(from: url)
        return try JSONDecoder().decode([Post].self, from: data)
```

```
    }
}
// ViewModel (Open/Closed Principle)
class PostViewModel: ObservableObject {
    @Published var posts: [Post] = []
    private let postService: PostServiceProtocol

    init(postService: PostServiceProtocol = PostService()) {
        self.postService = postService
    }

    func loadPosts() async {
        do {
            posts = try await postService.fetchPosts()
        } catch {
            print("Failed to load posts: \(error)")
        }
    }
}
// View
struct PostListView: View {
    @StateObject var viewModel = PostViewModel()

    var body: some View {
        List(viewModel.posts, id: \.id) { post in
            Text(post.title)
        }
        .task {
            await viewModel.loadPosts()
        }
    }
}
```

This approach follows:

☐ **S** - Single Responsibility: PostService only fetches data.

☐ **O** - Open/Closed: PostServiceProtocol allows easy extension.

☐ **D** - Dependency Inversion: PostViewModel depends on an **abstraction, not a concrete class**.

---

5. How do you create a custom SwiftUI modifier?

A **Custom Modifier** lets you reuse UI styles efficiently.

Example:

```
struct TitleModifier: ViewModifier {
```

```
func body(content: Content) -> some View {
    content
        .font(.headline)
        .foregroundColor(.blue)
        .padding()
    }
}
struct ContentView: View {
    var body: some View {
        Text("Hello, SwiftUI!")
            .modifier(TitleModifier()) // Applying custom modifier
    }
}
```

OR using .extension for cleaner code:

```
extension View {
    func titleStyle() -> some View {
        self.modifier(TitleModifier())
    }
}

Text("Hello, SwiftUI!").titleStyle()
```

---

6. What is LazyVStack and LazyHStack?

LazyVStack and LazyHStack efficiently load views **only when needed**, improving performance for large lists.

Example:

```
struct LazyStackExample: View {
    var body: some View {
        ScrollView {
            LazyVStack {
                ForEach(1...1000, id: \.self) { i in
                    Text("Item \(i)")
                        .padding()
                }
            }
        }
    }
}
```

---

7. How do you navigate between views in SwiftUI?

Use **NavigationStack** (iOS 16+) or **NavigationView** (iOS 15 &

below).

Example using NavigationStack:

```
struct HomeView: View {
    var body: some View {
        NavigationStack {
            NavigationLink("Go to Detail", destination: DetailView())
        }
    }
}

struct DetailView: View {
    var body: some View {
        Text("Detail Page")
    }
}
```

8. How do you show an alert in SwiftUI?

Use the .alert modifier.

```
struct AlertExample: View {
    @State private var showAlert = false

    var body: some View {
        Button("Show Alert") {
            showAlert = true
        }
        .alert("Hello SwiftUI!", isPresented: $showAlert) {
            Button("OK", role: .cancel) {}
        }
    }
}
```

9. How do you add a Tab Bar in SwiftUI?

Use TabView.

```
struct TabBarExample: View {
    var body: some View {
        TabView {
            Text("Home").tabItem { Label("Home", systemImage: "house") }
            Text("Profile").tabItem { Label("Profile", systemImage: "person") }
        }
    }
}
```

10. What is @AppStorage in SwiftUI?

@AppStorage provides an easy way to store **user preferences**.

Example:

```
struct SettingsView: View {
    @AppStorage("isDarkMode") private var isDarkMode = false

    var body: some View {
        Toggle("Dark Mode", isOn: $isDarkMode)
            .padding()
    }
}
```

SWIFTUI INTERVIEW Q&A (NON-CODING)

1. Why did Apple introduce SwiftUI?

Apple introduced SwiftUI to **simplify UI development** across all Apple platforms using a **declarative syntax**. Key reasons:

- **Less Boilerplate Code** – Eliminates complex delegate patterns from UIKit.
- **Live Previews** – Developers can see UI changes in real-time.
- **Cross-Platform** – Write once, run on iOS, macOS, watchOS, and tvOS.
- **Better State Management** – Uses property wrappers (@State, @Binding, @ObservedObject) instead of traditional delegation.

---

2. What are the key differences between declarative and imperative UI frameworks?

Feature	Declarative (SwiftUI)	Imperative (UIKit)
Approach	Describes **what** the UI should be	Defines **how** the UI should be built step-by-step
State Management	Uses @State, @Binding, @ObservedObject	Uses delegates, KVO, and NotificationCenter
UI Updates	Automatic (React-style reactivity)	Manual (reloadData(), setNeedsLayout())
Code Complexity	Less code, easy to read	More code, harder to maintain

Example:

- **SwiftUI:** Button("Click Me", action: { count += 1 })
- **UIKit:** button.addTarget(self, action: #selector(handleTap), for: .touchUpInside)

3. What are some challenges when migrating from UIKit to SwiftUI?

1. **Missing Features** – Not all UIKit components have direct SwiftUI counterparts (e.g., UICollectionView).
2. **Performance Concerns** – SwiftUI is not always optimized for complex animations or large datasets.
3. **Limited Backward Compatibility** – SwiftUI requires iOS 13+, meaning legacy apps may still need UIKit.
4. **Interoperability** – Some UIKit components (like AVPlayerViewController) need to be wrapped using UIViewControllerRepresentable.

4. What are View Modifiers in SwiftUI, and why are they useful?

View modifiers allow **reusable styling and behavior** without subclassing.

- **Encapsulation** – Group multiple modifications together (.font(), .foregroundColor(), .padding()).
- **Code Reusability** – Apply styles across different views.
- **Composition** – Can be chained for more complex UI.

Example Use Cases:

- Customizing text appearance (.titleStyle())
- Adding shadows, padding, or background styles

5. What are Lazy Stacks and Lazy Grids? Why are they important?

LazyVStack, LazyHStack, and LazyGrid **improve performance** by only rendering items **when needed**, instead of loading everything at once.

Benefits:

- Optimizes large lists (similar to UITableView).
- Reduces memory usage by creating views **only when scrolled into view.**
- Essential for handling thousands of items smoothly.

Common Mistake: Using VStack for large lists instead of LazyVStack, which loads all elements immediately.

---

6. What is the difference between @StateObject and @ObservedObject?

Both manage **observable objects**, but they serve different purposes.

Property Wrapper	When to Use	Persistence
@StateObject	When creating a **new instance** of an ObservableObject inside a view	Persists as long as the view exists
@ObservedObject	When **passing** an ObservableObject from a parent view	Recreated when view re-renders (loses state)

Example:

- Use @StateObject in **root** views.
- Use @ObservedObject when injecting a model **from a parent view**.

---

7. What is @EnvironmentObject, and when should you use it?

@EnvironmentObject is used for **global state sharing** across multiple views without explicitly passing data.

☐ **Best Use Cases:**

- Theme management (light/dark mode)
- Global user authentication state

- App-wide settings

☐ **Bad Use Cases:**

- Local data specific to a single view (use @State instead).

---

8. How does SwiftUI handle animations compared to UIKit?

SwiftUI provides a **declarative animation API**, eliminating the need for UIView.animate() or Core Animation.

Advantages:

- **Implicit Animations** – Automatically animates changes in properties like opacity or frame.
- **Explicit Animations** – Uses .animation() modifiers for full control.
- **Built-in Transitions** – slide, opacity, scale animations without extra code.

UIKit vs. SwiftUI Animation Example:

- **UIKit:** UIView.animate(withDuration: 0.5) { view.alpha = 0 }
- **SwiftUI:** .animation(.easeInOut(duration: 0.5))

---

9. What is the difference between @AppStorage and UserDefaults?

@AppStorage is a property wrapper for UserDefaults, simplifying **persistent data storage**.

Feature	@AppStorage	UserDefaults
Syntax	Cleaner (@AppStorage("key") var value = "")	More verbose (UserDefaults.standard.set(value, forKey: "key"))
Integration	Directly updates UI when value changes	Requires manual retrieval & UI updates

---

10. How do you optimize performance in SwiftUI?

1. **Use LazyVStack instead of VStack for long lists.**
2. **Minimize View Re-renders** – Avoid excessive use of @State.

3. **Use EquatableView** – Prevents unnecessary UI updates by comparing values.

4. **Optimize Image Loading** – Use AsyncImage for remote images.

5. **Reduce Computation in Views** – Move expensive calculations to a ViewModel.

11. Can SwiftUI work with UIKit? How?

Yes, SwiftUI and UIKit can **interoperate** using:

- UIViewControllerRepresentable – Wrap UIKit views inside SwiftUI.
- UIHostingController – Embed SwiftUI views inside UIKit apps.

Common Use Cases:

- Using WKWebView, AVPlayerViewController, or MKMapView in SwiftUI.
- Gradually migrating UIKit apps to SwiftUI without a full rewrite.

12. What are the different navigation options in SwiftUI?

1. **NavigationStack** (iOS 16+) – Recommended for complex navigation.
2. **NavigationLink** – Simple push navigation.
3. **TabView** – Bottom tab navigation.
4. **Sheet & FullScreenCover** – Presenting modals.
5. **Deep Linking** – Handling universal links via onOpenURL().

13. What is GeometryReader, and when should you use it?

GeometryReader provides access to a view's **size and position**.

Use Cases:

- Dynamic layouts that adapt to screen size.
- Creating **parallax effects** or custom animations.

- Measuring child view dimensions in SwiftUI.

⬜ **Caution:** Overuse can lead to unnecessary re-renders and layout calculations.

14. What is the recommended architecture for SwiftUI projects?

- **MVVM** – ⬜ Most common, separates UI & business logic.
- **Redux (TCA – The Composable Architecture)** – ⬜ Scalable for large apps, uses a single state container.
- **VIPER** – ⬜ Not a natural fit for SwiftUI.

15. What are some common mistakes developers make in SwiftUI?

⬜ Using VStack instead of LazyVStack for long lists.

⬜ Overusing @State when @Binding or @ObservedObject is needed.

⬜ Not optimizing navigation (NavigationLink inside List can cause performance issues).

⬜ Forgetting onDisappear() for memory cleanup.